I0750655

ISBN 978-0-9980711-2-1

Edited by Carley Gomez and Levi Sherman
Designed by Levi Sherman

A Partial Press publication
www.partialpress.net

A physical book which compiles conceptual books by various artists

A physical book which compiles conceptual books by various artists, possibly undermining their conceptual commitment to dematerialization, but also sparking unforeseen juxtapositions and insinuating the works into new situations.

Contents

Foreword
Carley Gomez
The Library 17

Reason

Bobby Lee
Mushroom book 29

Cathryn Miller/Byopia Press
Who Has Seen the Wind 30

Levi Sherman
Every Pair of Shoes I Own 31

Levi Sherman
Walk Book 32

Gabriel Sherman
Dictator's Handbook 33

derrais carter
Black Mess: A Visual Dictionary 34

Carol Freid
paper water clay heat 35

James Spyker
Read it or else 37

James Spyker
The Saskatchewan 38

VON WEIT HER(GEHOLT)
Life, Life-Size: Complete Collection 39

Mati
A word of advice from a supporting beam of the ruling class 40

Connor Frew
Functional Architecture 41

Bethany Johnson
Memory Loss 42

Lui Kohlmann
Supply Chain Encyclopedia 43

Nathanael Jones
44

Marcel Croxson
Eos 45

Cathryn Miller/Byopia Press
The Memory of Water 46

Nada Dreamer
Blind Date: Trickster Conversion of Psychosexual Anxiety into Archetypal Shadow Theatre 47

Annelyse Gelman
PET 48

Alex Hanson
The last copy of Techniques of Archaeological Excavation by Philip Barker 49

Catalina Kobelt
Stop Trying to Live Right 50

Rick Henry
Beyond Zeros 51

Bethanie Irons
s c r e e n r e a d e r 52

Constanze Kreiser
A Book on Jellyfish 53

S Cearley
Attrition Clause 55

Marnie Powers-Torrey
Nomad's Book 56

Katrina Petrauskas
Tempting Fate 57

Gabriel Sherman
I have seen the wind 58

Touch

Karla Zorrilla
Chapters 61

We Da Pepo
Patience is eating at me 62

Reba Elliott
Bead Maze Book 64

Will Mairs
Flürgstruurvenn (Book of Grief) 65

Eileen Ramos
Psychotic Break 66

Cathryn Miller/Byopia Press
Poems from the Dark 68

Susanna Harris
A Meditation in the Transfer of What Was to What Is 69

Vera Benschop
Glass Book 71

James Spyker
Clean After Reading 72

Evan Patrick Maloney
A Bird's Nest 73

Woody Leslie
Door Book 74

Marilyn Stablein
Walkabout: Chance Meanders 75

K.S. Ernst
Woof! 76

Andrew David King
Ghosts Should Pay Rent 77

Liz Oeftering
Out for Delivery 78

Andrew David King
Snowdrops 79

Florence Lanxuan Liu
The Sentiment Shall Remain 80

Andrew David King
Special Collections 81

Bruno Neiva
Open your book! 82

Monica The Creative Beast
Book of Shadows: Plagues of Humankind 83

Sarah Maker
Miles and Shoes 85

Marnie Powers-Torrey
Flipping Seats 86

Narges Porsandekhial
One hundred and forty to get there 88

Lisa Beth Robinson
Passage 89

Lesley Ruda
Drawing Inside: Hardcover Books of Unpulped Fiction 90

Kyla Anne Spencer
An accordion book (never ending). 91

Nanette Wylde
soul haiku 92

Memory

Maureen Alsop
TALLY HO ÉCRITURE FÉMININE MECHANIQUE 95

Abigail Guidry
Everything I never told you 97

Karen Carcia
Post of Ice 98

Ellen Bruex
An Index of Beginnings and Endings 99

Amandine Nabarra
Coma (deep sleep) 101

Ally Zlatar
This Body of Mine 102

Kristen Lyle
Just a Phase 104

Michael Hampton
Bibliophial 105

John Gialanella
The Other Guy 106

Marina Kassianidou
Hellos and Goodbyes 107

Judith Caroline Feist
How to make a book to forget someone you once loved. 108

Karin Falcone
Notebook Destroyed by Rainstorm 110

Bea Drysdale
Ben the Hoose 112

Meghan Marin
Hope this finds you well. 113

Connor Frew
There is no time for the book. 114

Connor Frew
New Edition 115

Andrew David King
Nervous System 116

Amandine Nabarra
Solastalgia 117

Mireille Ribière
Double-Edged 118

Linda Parr
Circumnavigation 119

ossa
The Book of Davron 121

Morgan Whitehead
Swell 122

M H
Made up of you since 1990 123

Lily Oliver
Appendage 124

Sue O'Donnell
Memory Study I 125

Sue O'Donnell
Memory Study II 126

Sue O'Donnell
Memory Study III 127

Claire B. Marcus
rePLACEments 128

Cathryn Miller/Byopia Press
The Barbie Pictorial History of Western Art 129

Vera Benschop
Interference 130

Merridawn Duckler
Big Book of Nothing 131

Levi Sherman
Extended Family 133

Imagination

Gwendolyn Paradice and Kyle Paradice
This is Not a Fairytale 137

Narges Porsandekhial
Nothing and Everything 138

Amanda D'Amico
The Future of the Past 139

Sumru Tekin
A Manual for Collecting in Three Chapters (as told to Ü) Or Impossible Directions/ Unnatural Disasters* 140

Peter and Donna Thomas
Ignited 142

Esther K Smith & Susan Happersett
Random Color Generated Instant Book 143

Marianne Dages
Dreamt I was reading The Book of Tides. 145

Nathanael Kooperkamp
Future Memory Photo Album 146

Safwat Saleem
The Self-Help Library 147

Esar Aadil
Dances of Great Contemplation 148

Sydney Anne Smith
make a book like a dog 149

John Clark
Nothing Will Ever Suffice (unsatisfactory working title for this realisation only) 150

Connor Frew
Rat King 151

E.L. Gamble
Genocide Incorporated 152

Shannon Davis
Wish You Were Here 153

Carley Gomez
Operation Bird Book 154

Andrew David King
Dickinson's Watch 155

Kyle Adam Kalev Peets
A List of Things You Could Be Doing Right Now Instead of Reading This Book 156

Alyssa Laurel Ringler
Wall Street 157

AB Gorham
UFO Song 158

Afterword
India Johnson
Guide to Mail Standards of the United States Postal Service Domestic Mail Manual (DMM) Section 170 161

Contributors 178

Foreword

Carley Gomez
The Library

I came across a library behind a dilapidated two-story house one afternoon while I was walking to the pharmacy around the corner from my mother's house. The library was red and square with gold letters on the sign out front. I couldn't remember it being there before, but it was possible that it was new or that I had missed it. My mother always thought that I was prone to moving through life looking inward instead of outward, and I had only returned to the area recently.

I always loved to read. I tended to buy new rather than used, but I knew that it was a bad habit. The dangers of accumulating had become evident when I began to clean out my mother's house after she died.

The library's red paint was the bright shine of lipstick, a luring color. It had been a while since I had time to read a novel. And since the funeral was over and all the arrangements were done with, I had a bit of time to look through some books. So I walked to its doors, leaves and small branches crunching beneath my sneakered feet.

When I stepped inside, I was met with the sight of one large room, lit by low sconces. In the front of the room, a woman sat at an information desk at the front. Behind her were tables and chairs of various shapes and sizes. There was no interior organization — if one hoarded furniture, I imagined this is what their home would look like. Odder still, there were no books. The walls were lined with wood paneling and not a single bookshelf stood against them. I looked for doorways or stairs that might lead to where the books were kept, but there were none.

Curious, I walked up to the woman at the desk as she stared intently through her glasses at nothing behind me.

"How can I help you?" she asked, still not looking at me. The blue in her eyes was flat like sky.

I chewed on the side of my tongue, my eyes flickering around the bare walls once more. "Are the books in another room?"

"Take a seat in the chair that calls to you. The books will be out soon." She looked down at the desk, clearly dismissing me.

I thought about leaving. But as I glanced at the tables and chairs, a plush armchair with blue stripes caught my eye. It looked so comfortable, and suddenly I felt dead on my feet. A few moments rest before finishing my errand and walking back to my mother's house couldn't hurt. I sat down and warmth suffused my limbs as the chair seemed to wrap around my body. My eyelids felt thick, and I drifted to sleep.

Later, I woke with a start. I blinked and saw that others had appeared in the library. Several men and women sat reading throughout the room. And on the table in front of me sat a square, brown book with gilded edges. I looked for the person who had delivered this volume, but the only woman working was still sitting at the information desk.

The book was warm when I picked it up to inspect it, as if someone had just held it in their arms. There was no title, nothing on the back, and the spine was blank except for the raised bands. I opened it, and the book itself was blank. Page after page was empty. I pressed my face deeper, looking for marks and, in breathing deep, I smelled something familiar. There was something with a hint of clay, like the earth underneath a school field, and something with the sting of lemon that had once wafted from my mother's skirts. I sucked deep, filling my lungs, warmth in my chest, but the scent faded. I turned the page, eager for more and inhaled again. This time drying pine needles and new plastic, a hint of warm molasses. Page after page I could smell my life — my school, my girlhood shame as I grew and changed, the wet woodchip smell of an old hamster, my brother at the turn of his addiction — the sour underneath the forest-clean scent.

At the end of the book, I tried to return to the beginning and start again but the scents were gone. The book was empty. I set it down, uncertain what to do. Nearby a woman with wide, expressive eyes laughed on a chaise lounge. A man across the room sat in a rocking chair and cried, his button-down shirt wrinkling around the roll of his shoulders. Feeling suddenly like an intruder, I stood up and walked out of the library, avoiding the eyes of the woman at the front of the room.

As soon as I reached the outdoors, I felt unstable, frightened. I looked at my cell phone and realized that hours had passed. My skin felt tight around my chest and the sidewalk felt tilted somehow.

I walked home, my errands forgotten, and I wondered if the library had been a hallucination. Books weren't made of smells. Libraries were orderly. Perhaps the stress of the funeral had brought on an episode. For two weeks, I avoided that street and moved on with my life, trying to ignore the book of scent.

But then one afternoon, I was distracted by thoughts of my mother's green eyes, of the hospital bills I still needed to deal with, of the way skin ages, and I ended up back beside the library on my walk to the train. The building was still a wet red. The windows were dark. I shouldn't have wanted to return. The shivering in my stomach should have led me away. But instead, I went back inside the library.

This time the room was crowded. People sat throughout in different chairs, but the blue striped one was empty. I went to it without looking at the woman at the front desk. I realized I did not trust her — it was very likely that she had been the one who'd given me the strange volume.

I sat and kept my eyes wide open, watching for the mysterious person that might be bringing in books. After several minutes, the only movement was people flipping pages. The walls were still blank. But then the small table in front of me started glowing with heat — and a book appeared on its surface.

It was a trick, it must've been. I glanced under the table but there was nothing there. I swung my head wildly around and everyone was enthralled within their own volumes. With shaking hands, I picked up the book.

The second book was a diary. The signature matched my mother's name — the scrawl a child's failing cursive. It was impossible, but I knew, I could feel it in my bones, that this was my mother's childhood diary.

I read my mother's cry. I read the sting of belt metal tear her skin. I read her shame when her communion dress ripped. I read her anger, her childhood feelings of injustice as her parents carved her like a doll while other children played freely in the street. I read the word savage and swallowed the bitter taste. I read her innocent hate. I read her desire for power, to teach others to fear her. I read love. I read racism. I read hope. I read mistakes. I read her humanness and wanted to throw it up out of me, and I tried to run from the chair, but it held me. The blue stripes sunk around me, enveloped me in warmth until I learned to breathe again.

This time on my way out, I confronted the librarian at the desk, my eyes burning from the anger of what I had learned.

"How are you doing this?" I demanded.

She looked above my head. "I don't do anything."

I wanted to grab her shoulders and shake her. "You're the only one working here."

Her eyes narrowed, but she still wouldn't look at me. "I am not."

"Who else works here?"

The question appeared to confuse her. She looked at me as if I was dense. "Well, the books, of course."

I laughed even though I didn't find her amusing at all. She disturbed me. I found the room unsettling. The longer I stood there, the more the air seemed to have a different flavor than outside. The dim lighting made me restless.

I ran outside, intending never to come back, but of course I returned.

The next book was filled with steam. It scalded my hand. I thought of my mother's ashes and the swirl of heat over the cups of coffee and condensed milk she made me when I was a child. I looked for blood on my hand from the chip she'd made in an outburst of anger.

The book after was a pop-up book. But nothing popped up, and each image was an empty window.

The next claimed to be a textbook. It called itself molecular biology, but the more I read, the more difficult it became to read. Soon the words were just gibberish, and I began to sob. So furious to not understand, so pitiful to be bested by words.

After, I thought I must've had a stroke and decided to make a doctor's appointment. But on the day I was scheduled to go, I went back to the library instead.

"Stop making me come here," I said to the librarian as I walked to my blue striped chair.

"What control have I?" she said crossly and looked at her blank desk.

The book that day was made of dust. I had no reason to believe it, or even to think it, but I swear it was from my own skin.

I lost sleep. I lost time. My freelance job I clung to, but I knew that if I didn't get my life together soon, I would lose that too. I told myself it was temporary. That I should just cook like normal, see friends as usual, go on errands as if I was living my regular life. But errands seemed pointless, friends had been lost as my mother was dying, and I could never cook well anyway. The library was daily. I hated it. I needed it.

The library gave me a children's book and painted me as a plot device. I was the clue that would lead the children home, and I was found wanting. They never found their cabin again.

Then there was a book with thousands of hands. I thought they were pictures, but as I flipped through, they began to move. Fingers wrapped themselves around my palm. Some released me quickly, others clung. I think some may have been praying. I think some wanted to stay, but the book wouldn't have it.

I watched a flipbook of my feet. I watched one of my father's eyes. One of my mother's hair. One of everything I've ever owned. I thought I would die after that one.

I read hundreds of books as days passed. Time was measured by them. The taste of my food was somehow measured by them too. I wondered if this was to be the pattern of my life.

One book turned into my childhood fish, Rick, and it fell to the floor, gasping and flopping. I watched it die in front of me, knowing that the library would never let me bring it to water. I cried for a week wondering what else the book would make me see.

There was a book of the sun, and I was temporarily blinded.

The good book came too, but the last page laughed at me.

I was brought a book with painted edges, and my hands became the color of moss, and everything I touched was made green with life for a long while — even the books that came after.

Then one day there was a book with a map. It showed no terrain. Instead, it counted steps and turns, and I knew that I must follow the directions. It walked me past my apartment, to the train. It listed the time to stay on the red line. It took me to a beach and bid me to unlace my shoes. It took me past the shallows of the lake and told me which stroke to use until I was in the middle of the water, small ripples and waves flowing between my fingers and toes.

There were no instructions for the way back. And I knew then, as my hair became a sheet in the water and the coolness pressed in on the heat of my raw, angry body, that I would never find the library again. That I would forever be lost in this lake, or I would forever be a small, pitiful person in a blue striped chair, even as my body worked, walked and slept in my mother's house, and performed the love and hate of life.

"The Library" first appeared in *Necessary Fiction*, November 13, 2019. *http://necessaryfiction.com/stories/CarleyGomezTheLibrary/*.

Reason

Bobby Lee
Mushroom book

Create a large batch of mushroom substrate using the appropriate nutrients based on your desired mushrooms. Pasteurize the mushroom substrate to kill any bacteria and unwanted mold. Inoculate the substrate with mushroom mycelium. Take some of the substrate and mix with fibrous material to compress into boards for book covers. Take the remaining substrate and compress into sheets of paper. Bind the mushroom substrate paper and book covers using your desired binding method. Fill the pages with writing or drawing — whatever you desire. These stories will feed the mushrooms. Once finished, place the mushroom book in a shallow grave loosely covered in moist soil, preferably in an area that receives a lot of moisture. Over time, and with the right conditions, the spores will draw nutrients from the book and grow into mushrooms.

Cathryn Miller/Byopia Press
Who Has Seen the Wind

A book of ninety-nine asemic poems.

The entire text consists of sonograms of the wind recorded at the same time for the same duration in the same location for ninety-nine days.

Levi Sherman

Every Pair of Shoes I Own

A pamphlet-stitched codex documenting every pair of shoes I own, printed directly from their inked soles. For each spread to contain a proper pair, I will wear mismatched shoes according to the imposition of the book's pages.

Levi Sherman

Walk Book

A meander book that documents a walk by unfolding in the cardinal directions taken by the walker. Visual or verbal notes may be added to the book.

Gabriel Sherman
Dictator's Handbook

Each page of the book is dedicated to a current or historical tyrant who has manipulated the media for their personal political or financial gain. The pages are woven carefully from newsprint, the warp being blank newsprint while the weft is composed of printed articles from respected newspapers. The articles relate to the respective politicians, but key words are woven behind the blank newsprint to create an alternative narrative. The new sentences that are created by obscuring the words are grammatically correct but tell an opposite or conflicting story. The obscured words represent explicit censorship but also the more subtle weaving of truth with fiction championed by dictators and their propagandists.

derrais carter

Black Mess: A Visual Dictionary

I am fascinated by the ways that Black theory and poetry converge in Douglas Kearney's incisive and humorous "Some Terms for Black Study." This lexicographical wonder is published in his collection *Mess and Mess and* (Noemi Press, 2015). "Some Terms for Black Study" contains fifty-nine concepts and definitions related to blackness and Black culture. Each entry works as a small poem and as an analytical concept that can be applied to other texts, ideas, and people. Collectively the piece functions, as the title suggests, as a dictionary for Black Study.

Here is a sample of Kearney's entries:

Blackness the condition of being the shit when it happens.

Code Switching when high-functioning / masochists mistake / their tongues for whips.

Post-Black I just (re)can't.

Uncle Tom a human shield / with no humans involved

My homage to Kearney's text is titled Black Mess. The book will be a pocket accordion-style visual dictionary filled with 11 × 17 in. broadsides for each entry.

Carol Freid

paper water clay heat

a book frozen in time by virtue of heat
a library made of clay books
a paper book made to be dipped
made to be dipped in paper clay
dipped in paper clay over & over & over
then once more
dip & dry & then dip again & dry
dip & dry
a dried dipped book
dry after being dipped
a paper book encased in paper clay encased
a book encased in clay air dried
bone dry
a book encased in paper clay to be fired
fired in a kiln
in a kiln that will be fired
fired to an orange yellow heat
1800 degrees Fahrenheit
dried clay book cold kiln
reaching maximum heat in twelve hours
slowly moving higher heat
heat moving water driven off like a hot breath
molecular water dissipated
organic materials burned away

bits of leaves butterfly wings carbon sulfur
clay particles fuse
firing slowly moving through sintering
moving from clay to ceramic
a book a ceramic book
a sealed solid book form
containing remnants of a fired paper book
a resting book a book resting on a shelf
dust of fired paper seeps out of unimagined openings
leaving a shadow
a shadow of dust
paper dust from a ceramic book

James Spyker
Read it or else

This structure encourages the reader to question whether they made the right choice to begin reading the book. It is software that the reader installs as a form of voluntary ransomware.

The text of the book is displayed one word at a time with an inappropriately long delay in between. At the end of each paragraph the user is required to retype the last word (still displayed on the screen) before continuing.

The software will have encrypted the contents of the hard drive when starting. Any attempt to stop reading the book partway will leave the contents encrypted. Once the reader has finished the book, the computer is safely returned to a working state.

It is important that the reader not be aware beforehand that this ransomware-like behavior will occur, but also that they be discouraged from buying the book. Any questions about the contents or book structure or any other element of the work should receive the reply "Although I would strongly discourage you from purchasing it, if you want to know, you'll need to buy the book."

This book structure is especially appropriate for writing that contains many articles, conjunctions, and prepositions.

James Spyker

The Saskatchewan

In early summer it takes 14 days (238 hours of sunlight) for water from melting snow in the Rockies to arrive in Saskatoon, getting a little warmer each town or city it passes through. Personal recollections have been collected from its route, each printed onto thin slabs of high thermal capacity wood.

These slabs are housed in a multi-layered, locked wooden box with hinges and extensions so that it unfolds into a model of the river system itself.

Atop the box is a solar panel powering tubes of cold and warm water controlling the temperature of each recollection.

To read this book, place it in a sunny location and wait for each recollection to reach the temperature corresponding to the expected temperature of the water at the corresponding location on the Ides of July (July 15th). The lock will then open.

It will be important to read the book relatively quickly so that it can be closed before the metal lock mechanisms have cooled/warmed enough to make the relocking impossible. If you do keep the book open too long, a technician can be sent to your location at your expense.

VON WEIT HER(GEHOLT)

Life, Life-Size: Complete Collection

Make a book that shows every animal on earth, life-size.

Mati

A word of advice from a supporting beam of the ruling class

Do not perceive what is rightfully not yours and make it double. I have a God to please and things I want from him. Therefore, I must take from your means of survival so I can live the good life.

Create a pocket and put cash in it. What does this mean to the politician? Write your answer on the cash.

Connor Frew
Functional Architecture

A handbook for the programs of architecture present in the video games Minecraft and Fortnite, including essays and criticism on how the horizons of non-material architectural practice sit in conversation with a global building ecology driven primarily by the accumulation of capital.

Bethany Johnson
Memory Loss

Background

According to the U.S. Environmental Protection Agency's reporting on solid waste disposal, approximately 640,000 tons of books are discarded in landfills in the United States each year. Using estimates for average book weight and thickness, this translates to roughly 320 million books, or 3,978 miles of shelved books.

As a point of reference, the Library of Congress, the world's largest library, contains approximately 838 miles of bookshelves. Another point of reference: the continental United States is 2,800 miles wide.

The Book

In one calendar year, assemble all books that would otherwise have been discarded in all US landfills. Line them up in a row as if on a single bookshelf and bind their spines together into one single continuous book. Lay the book's spine down on the ground; it will span the United States from the Pacific to the Atlantic. Let each end drape into the sea.

Lui Kohlmann

Supply Chain Encyclopedia

This open access, digital artists' book brings together investigative research, labor rights, IT, and artistic practice. It aggregates existing research about supply chains (featuring newspaper articles, scientific papers, and documentaries) and even does research of its own as an ongoing project. It enables workers to share their stories and document their working conditions.

A reader can search for a commodity or product to learn where and how it is produced and by which companies. Then the reader can follow the supply chain to see where and how that good is used, and by which companies, to create new products. Entries feature work conditions, labor rights, local policies, and broad sociological data, such as the average age, health conditions, and living conditions among the laborers. A subcategory features an open forum with ideas for civil protest and artistic interventions, ranging from formats for solo activists to large scale actions as well as resources for local workers and labor unions. This encyclopedia is a call to enact international solidarity with the global labor force.

Nathanael Jones

a procedure designed to translate the text of Olaudah Equiano's "The Interesting Narrative..." into a series of inharmonic keyboard drones, where the performance of this resulting score lasts as long as it takes the keyboardist to read Equiano's text

Marcel Croxson

Eos

Observe the colour of the dawn sky every morning for a year.

Record your findings on one sheet of paper each morning.

Bind these sheets together to form a 365-page Nomenclature of Colour.

Cathryn Miller/Byopia Press

The Memory of Water

A pictorial record of an installation piece.

The installation is created over a period of thirty days in winter at the edge of a northern lake.

The day before the installation commences, a sixty-two foot by two foot by two foot berm is built out of snow and a hole two feet by four feet is cut in the lake ice close to the shore.

Each day of the installation at six p.m., the newly formed ice is cut from the hole, the day's weather — previous night's low temperature, daytime high, hours of sunshine — is engraved on the sheet, and it is added to the berm in sequence.

Each day's "page" is photographed the following day as soon as there is sufficient light.

The finished book consists of all thirty images plus a fold-out image of the entire work.

Nada Dreamer

Blind Date: Trickster Conversion of Psychosexual Anxiety into Archetypal Shadow Theatre

In February of 2013, after happening upon a rebroadcast of an episode of the reality dating program *Blind Date* while experiencing severe jetlag resulting from attending an international conference of Jungian theoreticians (*Le Miraug Archetypee*), I sent an email to Sony — holders of the copyright for *Blind Date* — requesting that they provide all of the several hundred episodes to my research assistant so that we could begin working on a project which instantly confronted me with its necessity: cataloguing each episode through a detailed analysis of the journey undertaken by the daters, seen as a ritual offering of self to an uncertain trial for which they have volunteered for reasons relative to their particular universal-fragmentary roles. In the absence of a response, we chipped away at the task using the episodes available online, but they were insufficient for our goal of producing 1,681 pages (41 × 41, an essential number given Jung's proof that there are only 41 people alive on earth and the rest are either refracted spiritual holograms of those 41, or instead are mere shadow facade entities). The project soon died. Then, in March 2021, the email came; Sony was on board.

Annelyse Gelman

PET

A book of poems is integrated with an electronic game focused on caring for a digital pet, along the lines of Tamagotchi or Neopets. If the poems are not (at)tended to on a regular basis — opened, read — the pet gets sick, then dies, rendering the poems unreadable.

Alex Hanson

The last copy of Techniques of Archaeological Excavation by Philip Barker

The book *Techniques of Archaeological Excavation* by Philip Barker is, to date, the most detailed and extensive book on how to properly unearth something in a safe and reverent way. Authoritative and stimulating, the text was immediately hailed as the gold standard and is still one of the most widely used archeological field manuals.

The proposed book is the last copy of *Techniques of Archaeological Excavation* encased in a block of concrete.

The book/block is presented next to a jackhammer. The viewer is invited to attempt to access the book and information within.

Catalina Kobelt

Stop Trying to Live Right

The book combines a collection of social media videos with tips about how to do things the right way. On each page there is an illustrated reproduction of the footage, with flaps that have the annoying theme of the how-to video written on top (yes, using very subjective selection criteria). Under each flap you will find the tip, which in every case contains a variation on the only advice offered: "HOWEVER THE FUCK YOU WANT / HOWEVER THE FUCK YOU CAN."

Rick Henry
Beyond Zeros

The concept: the apocalypse, as in the devolution of a world to linguistic representation, to binary representation, to the ethereal, to absolute absence. This is performed on a 1,200-character text that begins with New Year's Eve 2001 and a George Harrison retrospective, as I sit for ten hours while tech support rewrites my new Gateway computer's hard drive to zeros. Along the way, a dozen reprieves from apocalypses dating from 753 BC. Along the way, Hamlet's problem is resolved. God's temper tantrums are effaced. Another philosophy to be lost to time. Indeed, "to be" is rendered moot.

The material: 1,200 sheets of paper, ink, vapor, vacuum

The layout: on the first page is the 1,200 character philosophy of the apocalypse

Thereafter, the text is reprinted, but with each page turn a character (including spaces and punctuation) is rewritten to a zero through the 1,200-page book,

as the text is rewritten to zeros, the story presented in the language changes, coalescing into several smaller but "coherent" texts (page 1,196 is a coherent "I am"),

as the text turns to zeros, the zeros become vapor,

as the text turns to zeros to vapor, the book becomes a vacuum...

Bethanie Irons

screenreader

a n a r t b o o k c o n s i s t i n g e n t i r e l
y o f a l t t e x t t o d e s c r i b e d i g i t a l
a r t n o p u n c t u a t i o n o r c a p i t a l l
e t t e r s w o u l d b e u s e d e v e r y c h a r
a c t e r o f a w o r d w o u l d h a v e a s p a
c e b e t w e e n s o t h a t r e a d e r s s p e n
d t i m e w i t h t h e t e x t c o l l a g e i t t
o g e t h e r a n d m a k e s e n s e o f h o w t
h e c h a r a c t e r s c r e a t e w o r d s a n d
m e a n i n g a s i f r e a d i n g a n d l o o k i
n g a n d s e e i n g f o r t h e f i r s t t i m e

Constanze Kreiser

A Book on Jellyfish

I love everything about the sea — the sand, the waves, the wind — even jellyfish. As a formalist I like their round shape and symmetries. They are pleasant to touch and they are beautiful to watch, with their patterns in bright fluoerescent colours. I adore their nearly invisible movements, functioning like a motorboat. And there is that lovely shape-changing while moving, in contrast to the geometric half sphere when floating at leisure.

Since I began making conceptual artists' books in 2013, I have wondered what form and material a book on jellyfish might take. I have not yet attempted this book because of technical reasons (which material to choose, which colour, which surface?) but also because I was unsure how to illustrate the topic: maybe with drawings or hyperrealisitc photographs or simple blind embossments? Maybe some mysterious thermochromic technique that shows pictures only when touched?

My interest is in its softness, its slippery surface, its mixture of transparent and opaque parts, its very long tentacles and hidden mouth. Maybe I should try to invent an artificial jellyfish in my kitchen and define a starter set for experiments? Or present jellyfish as a future food?

What kind of text would accompany the pictures or haptics? A scientific text to contrast with childlike linocuts? Something more lyric to accompany well-lit photographs? An environmental text showing the consequences of climate change, with drawings of deformed medusae species? Dark schemes on dark paper to match the lacking light of the deep sea?

Ideas start to float in my brain, and I enjoy the tickle of yet untouched territory. Probably this book will never be made. It will stay utopian and change shape now and then, like jellyfish do.

S Cearley
Attrition Clause

The book is a series of clear plastic sheets with printed text. Turning the first page removes some words, leaving behind the collection of others. It is reminiscent of the "visible man" sheets found in older encyclopedias. Each succeeding page, however, does not open up a new layer of the text, but the remaining words give the artist's statement for the piece proceeding. Each successive page turn strips away some of the text, leaving the next explanation of the work on the page before. Eventually the reader is left with the final blank space, the back of the book, to explain what they've read.

Marnie Powers-Torrey

Nomad's Book

This book of insulated, carbon-fiber panels formed from 100% post-consumer waste is carried with a shoulder strap. The hinges at the head, tail, spine, and fore-edge rotate 360 degrees and lock into place in thirty-degree increments, forming a seal. The book opens to form a variety of structures that keep the reader dry, cool in hot weather, and warm in cool weather. Hinges disengage so that the reader can arrange the panels for sleeping, eating, sitting, etc. The book is published in volumes of thirty, sixty, and ninety panels.

Katrina Petrauskas
Tempting Fate

Analog Version

Find an open call to publish a book.
Conceptualize a book.
Draft a proposal and fill out all necessary forms.
Mail your documents one day after the deadline.

Digital Version

Find an open call to publish a book.
Conceptualize a book.
Draft a proposal and fill out all necessary forms.
Submit your documents one minute after the deadline.

Gabriel Sherman

I have seen the wind

Choose around 20 locations of social, environmental, economic, personal, or scientific interest. Erect several 20 × 30 in. foam core boards 10 feet in the air and coat with a clear-drying adhesive that retains its stickiness for at least 24 hours. Collect the boards after they are 50–100% covered in items and particles deposited by the wind, monitoring for interesting patterns. Bind the foam core boards together. Don't forget to add a dust jacket.

Touch

Karla Zorrilla
Chapters

This book is between two; bodies, sides and dreams.

For a year, you and your partner will get bed sheets that you like for their texture, color, graphics, etc. Do this without sharing your choices or the number of sheets you have chosen.

On day 365, spread a white sheet on your bed; on it, place your sheets one by one, alternating one another's choices in complete silence. Make a simple seam down the middle and "close" the book.

Open the first page, each of you will choose a side and lie down on it. Sleep through the night and discuss the next day whether the pattern on your side influenced your dreams and thoughts. Turn a new page to sleep on when night falls. Do not change sides.

Repeat this action until you reach the middle of the book. Find that balance in sleeping together but apart. Continue to share your reading experiences and dreams. As the pages turn, one of you will have more support, the other less, until reaching the white end sheet.

We Da Pepo
Patience is eating at me

Materials:
1 terrarium
1 booklice colony
Your choice of paper
Water

Directions:
Add your hungry insects to the terrarium
Hold sheets of paper in the palms of your hands
Crumble the sheets into a tight ball
Reopen and flatten them out
Trace the creases left on the papers
Make a record of words around you along the lines traced
Write without stopping
Once the previous steps have been completed
spray the papers with water
Drop them into the terrarium
Place all ingredients in a dark humid corner
Spray water weekly
until the booklice eat them

Read the words with the trails the
booklice have left behind
Be patient
until time, words, trails blend into a story
Repeat to find more stories

Reba Elliott

Bead Maze Book

Do you remember that toy in the dentist's office? The one in the waiting room with curving and curling wires, where each wire was strung with wooden beads, and you were supposed to move the beads along the wires to the other end? This is a book with pages attached to a wire like that, a long wire that curves up and down and winds and loops and ends up at the other side of the room. To turn the pages, you have to move your whole body, sliding each page along the wires and across the space, sometimes lifting it up over your head, sometimes bending down almost to the ground to follow the curve of the wire, and then you have to walk back for the next page.

Will Mairs

Flürgstruurvenn (Book of Grief)

500 sheets of 11 × 17 in. paper, loose in a big, blue Ikea bag along with 500 stainless steel deck screws and a yellow screwdriver.

Eileen Ramos

Psychotic Break

It's hard to relay what psychosis is to someone neurotypical. Psychosis is a complete break from reality, where you hold beliefs that aren't possible at all. This is by no means exhaustive but offers a door ajar.

The book's versos are photos of each room in my home, the rectos are all black. A folder in the back contains transparencies — a different ink color, designated room, and year (2010/2012) — which you overlay on photos.

White — auditory hallucinations: Pat Sajak's taunts, commercials telling me to run.

Yellow — eyes on every piece of furniture with cameras livestreaming us.

Red — visual hallucinations: Cast of the Filipino soap opera "Legacy" acting out scenes from my life and what people are doing behind my back.

Purple — what I'm guilty of: car accidents, 9/11, US debt.

Green — what's occurring in reality, what's being said on TV, family conversations.

Orange — how my mind interprets the green, e.g. Wheel of Fortune answer is "PORK CHOPS." I panicked as my mom was cooking pork chops, and the TV was mocking us.

The transparencies will have drawings, photos, bullet points, bubbles, and flowchart arrows for how each delusion/hallucination impacts the other. Anything in bold ink indicates their return in 2012. Place these overlays over a black page to read them more easily. When piled together, you witness how these overwhelming false beliefs crushed me into catatonia.

Cathryn Miller/Byopia Press
Poems from the Dark

A book of asemic poetry.

The entire text of the book consists of reproductions of the patterns created by wood-boring insects, the intricate networks left just under the bark of the tree.

Susanna Harris

A Meditation in the Transfer of What Was to What Is

1. Start with papers that hold meaning to you, preferably that belonged to a loved one that has passed.
   A notebook
   A sketchbook
   A diary
   etc.
2. Prepare a space to safely burn these papers.
3. Burn the papers with intention and care, leaving only ash — preferably decent sized pieces of the ash.
4. Carefully collect the ash into a bag before wind or water render the ash unusable.
5. Prepare a clean space that can get dirty. Include a box of tissues in case of emotions.
6. Prepare a needle and thread; knot the end of the thread. Choose a thread color that is meaningful to you.
7. Empty the bag of ashes onto the clean surface.
8. With bare hands, gently work with the pieces of ash, looking through them and perhaps organizing them by size. Emotion is welcome.

9. Start to sew pieces together by stitching through the middle of each piece of ash. Not all of the ash will hold up through the process. Accept this loss; no material should be precious.
10. Tie off the thread at the other end of the stitched ash.
11. Clean up the space, releasing the remaining ash to the earth.

Vera Benschop

Glass Book

Get several (5–10) pieces of glass cut to the same size. (Frame shops do a great job of this; 5 × 7 in. is a good size.) Choose several images that can be easily translated into an engraving, something solid and not fragile, but maybe also soft. Keep in mind all images will be visible somewhat simultaneously. Add a title if you want. Have the images or text laser engraved into the glass. Perfect bind the book with cloth or leather and strong, flexible glue. Hot glue might work too, who knows. Sand the edges of the glass if it suits you. Be careful — now you have a glass book.

James Spyker
Clean After Reading

Sometimes you want your words and phrases to be lived with rather than just read. Printed on thin, opaque, fresh glycerin sheets using carbon-based ink, the pages are stacked and allowed to cure together to form usable bars of soap.

Given the nature of soaps, the author may choose a dos-a-dos format so that two different texts, starting on each side, meet in the middle. A single text may also be interesting, where the reader reads from both directions, eventually reaching the middle of the story.

A person could read this on their own as part of the normal soapish moments of their day. The books could also be available in a gallery space, where visitors would be invited to use the books. Each person would have to choose where to stop their own reading, creating the starting point for the next person.

It may be interesting to note that the use of carbon-based inks would likely take a certain amount of skill to master if the books are to leave you cleaner than you were before you started.

Evan Patrick Maloney

A Bird's Nest

Any bird's nest can be a book — put together with specific and various bits and bobs, carefully selected and arranged to meet the author's unique goals. The bird's nest is bound with longevity and usability in mind and is intentionally kept in the safest of places. A tree is its shelf, a forest its library. Every nest, assembled and bound, contains a story with a clear beginning, middle, and joyous or tragic end. Eventually the author moves on to make new nests and tell new stories, and while the old nest may look empty or abandoned, remnants of the tale it told remain. The bird's nest is a record of life lived; ingenuity, skill, and instinct come together to create a safe place for a fragile thing to grow. Every bird's nest can be a book, we need only read them.

Woody Leslie
Door Book

The book is the size of a door.

In fact, the book is a door. The book is suspended between two rooms. The front and back covers have doorknobs, and one side of the doorframe serves as the book's spine to which all the signatures are bound.

To enter the room you must read the book.

Marilyn Stablein

Walkabout: Chance Meanders

Make an interactive book object for a reader to play a game of chance and travel.

Objective: Explore destinations.

To Play: Open protective book cover to find a circular gameboard with two bands each divided into six wedges to make twelve featured spots. Spin the spinner in the center to begin.

1. The first spin points to the widest band featuring one of six city areas to explore: park, playground, neighborhood, shopping center, school, business district.
2. The second spin selects from the middle band, one of six attractions to explore: museum, gallery, theater, market, cafe, bakery.

Note: A player should not have a fixed destination in mind.

Winner: There is no winner in Walkabout.

K.S. Ernst

Woof!

A number of libraries have programs to encourage children to read. During these programs at the library the children read to a dog.

The idea is to design a book that would actually be interesting to the dog. The book would have simply worded pages that could be read to a dog by a child or adult at the library or at home. These pages would need to contain at least some words familiar to most dogs. The pages would be thick and heavy and would contain one or more of the following elements to entertain the dog:

- Scratch and sniff
- Squeaker
- Something embedded (a little handle? string?) in the pages that could be secretly moved by the reader while the dog watches
- Something embedded in the pages that would pop up/out

I can envision a similar book for cats, but it would have to be much more exciting for a cat to stick around.

Andrew David King
Ghosts Should Pay Rent

An artists' book consisting of two variations, both of which may be executed simultaneously. First variation: the book consists of a stamp-sized codex and a magnifying glass placed on the floor of a gutted, ground-level room, preferably with large windows and shaded by sycamores. The book is to be read sitting on the floor, alone, with the sonic accompaniment of bricks and chunks of concrete being thrown, without regularity, into a large dumpster outside. Second variation: the book consists of a codex up to several feet in height. The codex is held vertically by a machine so that its uppermost edge is roughly at the eye level of the reader, who is not permitted to touch it. The machine is placed in the hallway of an empty house that leads to an open field. The reader must take one step (or its equivalent) back to trigger the machine to turn the page. The reader must continue, backwards, into the field to reach the end of the book.

Liz Oeftering

Out for Delivery

An art book of illustrations, collage, and photo edits of actual photos of my food deliveries sent during the pandemic by no-contact delivery drivers.

Andrew David King
Snowdrops

A multi-stage artists' book consisting of rubbings, in any order and without page numbers, of the roughly 1,000 Stolpersteine in Vienna. The Stolpersteine (stumbling stones) are metal plaques bearing the names and dates of individuals deported and murdered in the Holocaust, embedded in the sidewalks at their last known place of residence. Although the book conceptually consists of rubbings of every Stolpersteine in the city, it may be instantiated partially, even by a single rubbing; and a once-complete version of *Snowdrops* may be rendered incomplete by the installation of new Stolpersteine. Only one version, complete or incomplete, of *Snowdrops* may exist at one time. The rubbings of each new version are created on that day's newspaper using the ashes of the previous version. If these prove insufficient (and to create the first version of the project), ashes from the burned works of Else Feldmann, Egon Friedell, Peter Hammerschlag, Julius Klinger, Fritz Löhner-Beda, Jura Soyfer, and David Vogel — Viennese writers murdered in the Holocaust — or works about them may be used. *Snowdrops* concludes when the author of its most recent version buries the text in a flowerbed.

Florence Lanxuan Liu

The Sentiment Shall Remain

Stain a page with body fluids. Fold. Seal.

Andrew David King
Special Collections

An artists' book created only when a reader requests to view it. After a request is made, the book — combining historical images with images made the day of its creation — is assembled several days prior to its viewing. If the reader must reschedule their visit before the book is made, then a different book is created for the new date; if the reader must reschedule after the first book has been made, it is destroyed and a new one created. To read the book, the reader must put on protective fabric gloves that have been freshly coated with black letterpress ink. After the book is read for the first time, it is allowed to dry and entered into the catalog. It can be read by anyone else subsequently so long as protective fabric gloves are worn.

Bruno Neiva

Open your book!

Don't judge a book by its pages!

Taking the cue from colouring books for adults and their therapeutic properties, *Open your book!* is an unopened book with uncut, blank pages, especially designed for you to relax, with ease of use and guaranteed effectiveness. Whenever you're feeling stressed or anxious, all you need to do to pull yourself back together is to rip open a few pages with your bare hands.

Monica The Creative Beast

Book of Shadows: Plagues of Humankind

The book is completely white — white covers and white pages. It appears to be a blank book until you take it into your hands. Slowly the title "Book of Shadows: Plagues of Humankind" appears and then disappears.

You turn blank white pages until a shadow materializes into a word and moves across the pages, from left to right. Then the word disappears.

There is one word for each page spread in the book, as if each spread is a new chapter.

The words, or chapters, that float across the pages begin as follows:

Inequality
Prejudice
Greed
Selfish
Racism
Ugly
Bitch
Poverty
Millionaire
Abuser
Fucker
Bigot

Coward
Slut
Worthless
Bastard
Crazy
Self-Centered
Asshole
Biased
Nationalism
Martyr
Nobody
Bully

With each turn of the page, the book absorbs your energy and randomly generates more shadow words that stem from your own subconscious, from deeply embedded messages you've received since childhood.

When you put the book down, it becomes blank again, awaiting the next "reader."

Sarah Maker

Miles and Shoes

This is a book you can literally climb inside and experience with all of your many senses: sight, hearing, taste, touch, smell, proprioception, equilibrioception, thermoception, and nociception. You are the main character, experiencing the life of another human with your eyes fully open. It is a story about wonder; excitement; boredom; fear and its twin, anger; gardening; and, always, love.

Marnie Powers-Torrey
Flipping Seats

Stage* set with circle of gray ovals, lit centrally.

Twelve figures wearing gray suits enter intermittently from each wing. Each wears shoes that clack, thud, or squeak and walks around circle clockwise, until finding seat. Each stoops for oval, takes seat, facing inward, and dons oval as mask.

Once ovals are claimed, figure enters from right and walks clockwise, tapping head of each seated figure. At half past hour, figure stops, turns around, and walks counterclockwise, head-tapping as they pass. When reaching quarter 'til, figure halts and turns inward.

Seated figure in front of halted figure stands, removes mask, and places it on halted figure who takes a seat. Standing figure walks clockwise, head-tapping, halts at quarter after, turns around, and walks counter clockwise, tapping, until reaching half past. Seated figure stands, masks standing figure who sits, and walks circle clockwise. Pattern repeats.

*alternatively, performance might be realized in book form, where pages becomes stages and activity is enacted through structure, materiality, production modality, page flipping, etc. For example, the theatre could be a fan book of narrow, transparent, flag-like pages that, when spiraled open, reveal one-inch dots printed one per page, beginning at the screw post binding and, slowing, radiating outward to form concentric circles when book is fully open. Periodically, empty pages appear to indicate vacated seats. Clacks, thuds, squeaks, and taps would be represented by various, visually textured strips made at the foredge side of each dot, one to two on each page to indicate the passing, seating, or felling of the figure as pages are turned. A crinkly transparent material would be placed between each of the pages, making noise when in motion. The postscript or colophon would include the above text, documentation of any live performance, and key for visual elements.

Narges Porsandekhial

One hundred and forty to get there

Imagine a giant book, maybe the size of a typical room. You enter the room and encounter the gigantic book. Enormous pages, each bigger than you. To turn each page, you have to move across the room and treat the papers, which are quite thin and soft, carefully.

The book has 70 pages and narrates a 140-character long poem. Each word of the poem is printed on a page, in alternating positions: the first word on the top of the first page, the second word on the bottom of the second page, and so on.

In this way, the reader needs to walk through the whole room in order to read the next word of the poem. After finishing the book — if anyone can — the challenge will be remembering anything from the poem.

Lisa Beth Robinson

Passage

This kinetic, interactive book is in a public park. Imagine a cast metal Jacob's ladder structure with metal banding straps for ribbons, whose boards (approximately 3.5 feet high, 8 feet long, and 8 feet deep) are mounted on rods that move in in-ground tracks. It is fluid enough that children can turn the pages, and works even better when multiple readers move the boards together. Pegs on the corners of the boards prevent possible accidents.

The text hides and reveals a local legend or a regional poet's poem. Language used employs the fulcrum of the structure to create twists in plot points or shifts in emotion.

Lesley Ruda

Drawing Inside: Hardcover Books of Unpulped Fiction

January, 2022

Take a solid wood cylinder, four inches in diameter, about two feet long, each end perpendicular to the length. Saw across the middle at any angle, making an ellipse on each side of the cut. These sections are your two hard copies.

Sand the wood smooth to the touch. Carefully gesso the four cut ends. They are the first and last pages of each book. Are the books a set, Part I and II? Visualize the wonders that embody the infinite pages between the two ends — like a CAT scan or slices of Wonder Bread. Then commit! Write or draw your first and last pages. Feel free to saw a few notches into the side of the cylinder, which is now your book cover. Cover design is personal, but plain wood grain lends arboreal poignancy and gravitas to this impulpable genre.

To edit, you need only reach for sandpaper or empty mind to start over.

At last! Books that stand tall on any coffee table or artist's block. They also recline, even roll, to display the first and last pages simultaneously, perfect for those who hate to bore through a whole book to get to the end.

Kyla Anne Spencer
An accordion book (never ending).

An accordion book (never ending).

Each page: overflowing with my love for you.

Nanette Wylde

soul haiku

(A slight volume of undisclosed materials
found where least expected)

Upon being lifted, the book notes the
current environmental conditions.

The book registers the touch of the reader — hand
size, texture, temperature, care in handling.

As the reader opens the cover to view the title page, the
book peers into the reader's eyes, reading the reader.

The reader turns the page to find the first line of a haiku,
which the book has written for this singular moment.

Turning the page again, the book adjusts and connects
to the reader's history and mindset, offering the
haiku's second line, specific to this reader.

The third page turn reveals the third line — a marvel of
exactitude and insight which will resonate with the reader,
once the book is closed and returned to its resting place.

Afterwards, year upon year, when conditions are
right, the poem will be remembered, considered,
thought to be the original. Yet with each remembrance
it will be new, revised for the reader's situation,
though the reader will never find that book again.

Memory

Maureen Alsop

TALLY HO
ÉCRITURE FÉMININE MECHANIQUE

I told you to smoke the three-layer cigars daily. "Smoke them, but don't be afraid to give them away," I said. I said "Definitely, share them when a baby is born."

The ash and the remaining cigar boxes are a book. A safety pin, a photo of your sister in a prom dress, rusted bottle caps, and a few letters are stored under the factory painted on a cedar wood lid. Yes, maybe it also holds marbles, a seashell, lost earrings, a dead bird, or a wallaby's skull. If you're lucky you'll hear a buzz-saw, catch the wind over the lake, and peer through silverfish and cicadas to see the seaweed and the trout frozen beneath ice.

Écriture feminine mechanics arise as they've always risen, in resistance. You've written parallel acts in cyclical slips, stream of consciousness, and fragments. You've burnt traditional constructions. Now you've been given a private dusk, a memento mori. The composition is an ephemeral object, somatic by design, crafted with intuition, sublimation, surrender.

Beyond language, the writing and art exist as a rough erotic. As talisman. Interpersonal in ruptures and syntax, soft in their discomforts. The book is an interrupted line of thought. Just as you are. It is a conventional architecture of narrative if you read closely: plot, character, conjuration. But you've always lived with the illegible, the lawless, so you wade through the brittle grass in midsummer. You divert from the line. You come seeking. If an intersection exists, a trinity of place or time or incident, it lives just under the skin. You touch it. You lose it.

Sensuality is a moment of recognition: the self and the subconscious communicate, the moment one's eyes open in the dark for the sake of the dark.

In sickness, in a lie, with one clean hand holding the ghost at the door and with one hand deep into the press of the horizon, a person can change. Snow can unzip the sky like a dress. Someone can call you home, can speak to you like a floodlight between the trees. A person can lie down, either in peace or in anguish, or both and in full desire of it all, not get up.

Abigail Guidry

Everything I never told you

Everything I've never spoken aloud, handwritten in ink made from violets on Spanish moss paper.

Loosely bound, twenty-four signatures so far.

Each signature is folded and written over the course of the year, and is stitched to the book on October twenty-third.

No covers; handle with care.

Once it is written, it is no longer speakable.

Once it has happened, it is written.

Karen Carcia

Post of Ice

The text of the book contains all the things you want to remember and some of the things you can't forget. Typeset by placing thin, raised letters (these could be metal or plastic) in a long, shallow, rectangular pan. Also place five nails upright in the pan to create sewing stations. Pour water over the letters and freeze. Create as many ice sheets as pages you want in your book. Once all the pages are frozen, lift the pages away from the type and remove the nails (this may take practice or the use of a thin tool to help pry the letters and nails away from the ice). Quickly sew the book together with thread. The book should be placed on a pedestal to be read. The book, like our memories, will change over time, become lovely, sad. It will crack and return to water. It will spill over the pedestal, out into the room. It will become only a memory, a little thread.

Ellen Bruex

An Index of Beginnings and Endings

BEGIN.

Materials:

Index cards — any color, store-bought or hand-made

Writing utensil — for documentation

Awareness of dates — for record-keeping

Ethnographic lens — focused on your own experiences

Time commitment:

Variable — one week to lifelong
(consistent documentation on a daily to weekly basis
is recommended)

Instructions:

Move through your days with awareness of new beginnings and final endings. Every time you experience a beginning, date-stamp an index card and write your beginning. Place the index card in the "beginnings" file. Keep it safe until you are ready to complete the project. Do the same with endings.

Beginnings (examples):
10-23-21: Started wearing red lipstick

12-03-21: Hello Charles, Dane, Karmen, Sam, Julia

01-29-22: Wrote my first love poem

Endings (examples):
08-20-21: The last night I slept in our bed

10-13-21: The lightbulb above the shower finally burnt out

02-25-22: Finished our mural

Binding:
Binding style is up to the author, and is optional.

END.

BEGIN.

END.

BEGIN AGAIN.

EVER END.

NEVER ENDING.

Amandine Nabarra

Coma (deep sleep)

My stepmother left us after going into a coma for the second time. When the doctors assured us there was no hope, we agreed to take her off the respiratory machine. I still feel guilty. I started an artists' book about her loss, but I couldn't finish it. Losing a loved one is being awash in the long and painful process of grieving.

I set this project aside since there were structural problems, and I couldn't face her death yet. I portrayed her floating in gauze as if she was still in a coma. I chose to make a collage with an old black and white image of her looking straight at the photographer. She was in her twenties, smiling. She looked so alive.

For more than a year, we have witnessed the ravages of COVID-19. Like me, many families have had to make difficult choices, often without being able to say goodbye to their loved ones. I know their pain; even after several years I feel it from time to time.

I'm still wondering if maybe I need to make peace with my own death? Or maybe I need to invent a way to let them know they're in our thoughts still, and forever.

Ally Zlatar
This Body of Mine

When a house is no longer a home.
The fire goes out. (Turn page)
When a body becomes violated.
It becomes a hollow shell. (Turn page)

You think about how much you have suffered, and how much you endured

~Pause~

When a house is no longer a home, and you can't
afford rent anywhere else. What do you do?
You stay.
You sit at the table and stare at the
remnants of ash in the fireplace.

(Turn Page)

When a body is violated, you can't buy a
new body. So, what do you do?
You stay in your body and stare at the remnants
of trauma that left its scars on you.

You think this author clearly went through some shit

(Turn Page)

A house that is no longer a home, a body that is no longer theirs — a shared struggle of endurance. How can we move forward when a place of refuge is no longer safe?

We can't.

(Closes Book)

You think about this book for two minutes then move on with the rest of your life

Kristen Lyle

Just a Phase

A book of images of the full moon, photographed each month during the year 2019.

In January of 2019 I decided to photograph every full moon of the coming year. I had just graduated art school and was already missing a consistent creative practice. In a year that was otherwise full of personal turbulence and ambiguity, photographing each full moon gave me something consistent to look forward to, plan for, and execute with intention. I planned to make a book of these images.

The photographs would be printed with historical photo printing methods (cyanotype and salt printing). The book would open with a one-page description of the project and then each successive spread would be dedicated to one month of the year. Photos would be tipped in so that the images themselves could be removed. I would include personal anecdotes, tarot cards, and other ephemera about the progression of the year. Thus, the "phases" would be more about my own progression since the moon (in its full phase every month) would appear very similar in each image.

This is the closest this book has come to completion.

Michael Hampton
Bibliophial

Introduction: Our planet was born of meteoric collision, clash, a geologically impure, complex entity that spins on its own axis as it gyrates round the sun. From collision, contamination and deformation ensued, perhaps even the blueprint of future doom.

Sammelbände: As the pre-Gutenberg scribal era adapted to movable type technology, early modern printers often combined generically diverse material in one binding, their customer an assembleur/author of loose sheets. Compilation was thus entwined with textual production.

Variable inventory (cardboard file box 2 × 22 × 33 cm): Expired reader's ID for the Wellcome Library/Selection of publishers' flyers/Bookmark/Quill/Stapled Report on Knowledge, ISBN 9781910055045/Handwritten rejection letter/Book review newspaper cutting/Artist's poster/Exhibition guide/Warning to thieves/Stapled facsimile Adana instruction manual Printing for the Million/Gummed Ex libris/COVID-19 desk reservation card for the British Library.

Further reading: Knight, Jeffrey T., *Bound to Read* (Philadelphia, PN: University of Pennsylvania Press, 2013)

John Gialanella

The Other Guy

There were six lunar landings from the mid-sixties to the early seventies, during the height of the Space Race. Twelve men stepped foot on the moon, but eighteen total were on those missions. Each Apollo mission carried three men into orbit, but only two made the trip from the command module in the lunar module to the surface of the moon, while one poor, lonely, forgotten fella was stuck babysitting the spaceship orbiting the moon. Shepard, Aldrin, Armstrong became household names. This book will honor Collins, Roosa, Gordon, et al. as "The Other Guy."

Other considerations:

The book could be specific to the lunar landings, or it could branch out to include other forgotten figures from famous and historic events.

Marina Kassianidou
Hellos and Goodbyes

A book containing the first and last phrases everyone important in my life has told me: the first phrase they said the first time we met and the last phrase they said the last time we met. Each encounter takes up a spread: the first phrase on the verso, the last phrase on the recto; the book's gutter silently encompassing the entire relationship.

The work necessitates recording the first phrase spoken to me by every person — as I cannot know in advance what that person's importance might be — and the last phrase they say every time we meet — as it is impossible to know which of our encounters will be the last. Every new last phrase will lead to the erasure of the previous last phrase. The work also necessitates defining importance, something that can only be done retroactively. It may already be too late to start this book. Or perhaps an additional parameter can be added — a book containing the first and last phrases everyone important in my life has told or will tell me starting today.

Necessarily, the book will be edited and printed posthumously. A second option is time travel.

Judith Caroline Feist

How to make a book to forget someone you once loved.

What you need:

Article of clothing that once belonged to someone you loved.

Any variety of paper (copy paper, newspaper, tissue paper, handmade paper — nothing glossy). You choose how many pages.

Writing utensil (preferably a pencil — carpenter).

Twine, natural yarn, rope, jute to use for tying.

Matches.

Shovel (unless you want to use your hands, which would be more personal).

Instructions:

Rip or cut article of clothing into similarly sized pieces. Does not matter how many. Don't throw anything away. Use all of the fabric.

On each piece of paper write down a sentence you wish you had said to the person who owned the now-destroyed article of clothing.

Set the fabric pieces in between the written notes. Make a fabric-note sandwich.

Tie the yarn/jute/misc. material around this bundle. Wrap it as many times as you can to utilize all the material.

Dig a hole. Put this bundle in the hole.

Strike match and light bundle in as many places as possible. Use as many matches as you can. If you run out, do not continue to attempt to light bundle on fire.

Let bundle burn to ashes.

Cover ashes (or unburned bundle) with dirt previously removed from hole.

Step on pile of dirt to flatten.

Walk away.

Karin Falcone

Notebook Destroyed by Rainstorm

Materials:

A small softcover notebook of about 48 pages.

Pilot G-2 or other water-based ink pens of varied colors.

Time:

One moon cycle plus a few days

Instructions:

Fill the notebook with observations, ideas, images from dreams, reading notes, lists and morning pages.*

Take one moon cycle to fill the notebook.

Leave your notebook outdoors during
a period of wind and rain.

Allow the storm to wash away your neuroses.

Retrieve the notebook and read it.

Notice where the elements created new conditions.

Notice where the mundane was
elevated by chance operations.

Notice where the random revealed your true intentions.

Recopy any exciting juxtapositions.

Invite future collaborations with
forces beyond your control.

Enjoy the watercolors in between.

*

"Morning Pages are three pages of longhand, stream of consciousness writing, done first thing in the morning ... Morning Pages provoke, clarify, comfort, cajole, prioritize and synchronize the day at hand."

— Julia Cameron, *The Artist's Way*

Bea Drysdale

Ben the Hoose

When staying in your parents' house, make a simple pamphlet with plain paper. On each page, draw a still life of objects that belong to your dad. Draw objects that have a special luminosity, or poignancy, because he is in hospital dying of a stroke. Work slowly. Aim for representation, with a good pencil, bearing in mind what Ruskin said — that drawing is shape and tone. Draw his reading lamp tied with string to the headboard of his bed. Draw the small stack of books at his bedside: Langston Hughes, Joseph Conrad, his diary. Draw his watch folded casually on the top book. Draw his boots under a side table in the sitting room, one toe hidden under the couch. Draw the calendar in the kitchen, open to a view of Glencoe, October 2020. Draw this poem taped to the fridge: "That is the land of lost content / I see it shining plain..." And so on. Do this in terror of the next video call from the hospital (these are Covid times, and they won't let you in), when he might yell, at his wit's end, for his son who died young, "Robert! Robert!" because you are useless; or he might end with an absurdly jaunty "Ciao ciao!"

Meghan Marin
Hope this finds you well.

I dig out my high school senior yearbook. I want to photograph everyone in my class, presented in alphabetical order. I get on Facebook and read up on my old classmates as if I haven't done it recently, just for entertainment. I make an Excel sheet of names, addresses, ideas for shots. I decide to photograph the members of my group chat of high school friends first because it's less awkward.

I don't remember everyone. I decide to leave their pages blank. For the people who ghost my request, I photograph something that reminds me of them. For Aaron, the karate school where I would fake having to pee to get out of sparring with him. I photograph Sarah with her child, who she has with the boy I dated in sixth and eighth grade. I go ice fishing with a boy who used to harass me on Twitter for being a feminist. He is balding now. It takes a year and twelve trips back home.

I decide to include personal anecdotes about each person in an index in the back. The final book is baby blue with gold inlaid text in a serif font — regal enough and reminiscent of our school colors. There are 147 pages for each of the 147 people I went to school with. When it is done, I think that I may repeat the project upon each passing decade.

Connor Frew

There is no time for the book.

Long-form interviews with friends, community, loved ones, about rent troubles, difficulties in housing, stresses from their job, grief and solidarity-laden conversation around the untenability of meaningful creative work under capitalism. There is no time for the book.

Connor Frew

New Edition

A series of artist statements collected after the end of the world.

Andrew David King

Nervous System

The reader first removes a tile from the floor, revealing a roughly-hewn concrete bunker containing a burlap sack covered in dirt. She places the sack on a nearby metal table accompanied by a single chair, where she may sit. From the burlap sack, the reader removes two objects. The first is a facsimile reprint of Edgar Kupfer-Koberwitz's diaries, written at, buried in, and excavated from Dachau, made to scale, with all references to dates, times, and days of the week redacted with permanent marker. The pages of the facsimile have been bound to a cylindrical spine without front or back cover; the book behaves something like a Rolodex turned on its side. The codex is accompanied by a taped narration of the diaries by a Dachau survivor, or child of a Dachau survivor, and a cassette player with which to play it. The second object is half of an iron supplement in a small paper envelope. To begin reading, the reader — health permitting — places the iron supplement on her tongue, not swallowing it for the duration of her engagement with the text. She chooses her starting point and reads in any direction and manner. The book is concluded when the reader no longer tastes blood in her mouth.

Amandine Nabarra

Solastalgia

A combination of the Latin solacium (comfort) and the Greek algia (pain) — to describe the anguish people feel when the place they live is under threat.

How to express the fears and disorientation of living in a world in mutation.

A faceted stone that would open and show an imaginary mental map. A collage of photos reminiscent of memories or dreams.

Mireille Ribière

Double-Edged

Premise of the book: imagine that, rummaging through a box of sundry photographs at a second-hand market, you come across photographic prints cut into vertical strips. Going through those strips, you realize that none of them are perfect matches, although a few appear to originate from different parts of the same print or from the same set. In all instances, crucial visual information seems to be missing from the strips. It looks as though the central sections of the original prints have been systematically cut out and either kept back or discarded separately.

Having selected images from your own archives or other sources, cut out the central part of each, so as to be left with two narrow vertical strips of varying sizes. Choose matching or contrasting strips that challenge the imagination when viewed together. Design a saddle-stitched book made of double-page spreads. Place one strip on the left side of each spread, and another on the right side, leaving a wide blank space in the gutter. Ask readers to fill in the blank spaces between the two strips with drawings or text, so as to create connections between the two partial images.

Linda Parr

Circumnavigation

2020 Vision put out a call in 2019 asking for artists' books about Magellan's voyage of discovery, to celebrate the first circumnavigation of the world five hundred years before.

OK, I thought, I can do this. I'm a seasoned artists' book maker, I can respond to any topic. So, I read around the subject and planned and plotted.

Portuguese Ferdinand Magellan had already voyaged east to the Spice Islands (now Indonesia) and back, via the Cape of Good Hope and the Indian Ocean. Then he planned and led a new expedition westward, an armada of five ships sponsored by King Charles I of Spain. He discovered his eponymous Strait through the tips of Chile and Argentina into the Pacific Ocean after a difficult and mutinous journey. He reached the Philippines, thus completing the first personal circumnavigation, but was killed in a battle with the local people. A captain of Basque origin, Juan Sebastián Elcano, then safely navigated home in the carrack Victoria, the only ship to complete the voyage.

I researched and drew old flags but realized that they would mean nothing to the modern reader. I collected images of ships, I drew ships, I etched ships. I bought fabric printed with ancient maps to make custom book cloth, and lost it (it must be somewhere). I visited the maritime museum in Bilbao where they celebrate Elcano, and I photographed the monuments to Magellan in Lisbon.

I found a format that would look good both in display on a shelf or in a cabinet, a double aspect 11 cm square, seven-page concertina with a 45 degree turn in the middle. Screen printed with hardcover, and sturdy Somerset paper to support the structure. Elegant, simple, clever; Magellan opened one way, Elcano the return, ocean map on the back.

History, and the wealth of his sponsor, have given Magellan all the posthumous fame, but it seems to me that he ran two separate half-marathons and had the misfortune to die during the second. Elcano and the Victoria certainly completed the marathon. Spain and Portugal have only recently patched things up. When the pandemic started its own travel, this project missed the quincentennial boat in 2019, and it seems that few have heard of Elcano reaching home in 1522.

So, this is my book, entirely conceptual, a fully worked up concept that never left the drawing board. It remains conceptual for practical reasons; it's past its sell-by date, or was it a best-before date?

ossa

The Book of Davron

An obscure and re-emerging corporation, Davron Global Services, has invested part of its profits into a collection of upcoming NFTs. At the end of a splendid quarter, the board of executives decides to publish the collection catalogue, to celebrate themselves and corporate patronage.

Aware of the unmemorable corporate printing landscape, they decide to letterpress print the catalogue on rag paper and vellum, in symbolic dialogue with Gutenberg's archetypal Bible.

Each NFT is represented solely by its metadata rather than the artwork's image; a descriptive file, hosted and forgotten on the InterPlanetary File System, that includes information on the artwork it is associated with — the creator, digital location, etc. The typeface of the catalogue is Typewriter No. 4 (Monotype 127), to imitate programming language.

Metadata is information for machines and slow, manual letterpress printing is aesthetic for humans; in their coming together, material and immaterial, analogue and digital are reunited. Layers and layers of information are added on top of each other, and the catalogue — and once again Davron Global Services and its board of executives — will be memorable.

Morgan Whitehead
Swell

As part of an ongoing project called *The Immaterial Archive*, the first publication comprises a series of autobiographical editions entitled *Swell*. Each chapter of my life is written, from the beginning, with each subsequent edition including the previous chapter. The editions, or additions, grow and grow, ad infinitum.

M H

Made up of you since 1990

In this book you'll discover the author adapting and mirroring other's patterns. How you view her is more important than how she views you.

More than three decades in, and she's fighting to break the mirrors within the pages of this book.

Lily Oliver

Appendage[1]

At the apex of a house there is a crawl space —
minuscule and ripe with heat inside
that crawl space is a small chrome camera

And on that camera is a single photo
evidence of evidence:
an eleven-year-old's bra, baby
pink, with monkeys on it — a hand-me-
down from the neighbors,
for when she actually needs it.

There is no knob in the door, just a surprised questioning 'O'.

---

1 You've read this one before. In the felted blue blacks near the inside of a body. The measured undressing of a story. A shutter releasing silently like a freckle coming to bloom.

Sue O'Donnell
Memory Study I

Take a road trip to visit every place you have ever lived. Document each location and include written recollections from each location. Establish a timeline that places each location chronologically. Research current events from the time you lived there (e.g., who was president, major discoveries, world events, etc.). If possible, locate photographs taken when you lived at that location and reenact the photograph. This may require reconnecting with neighbors and long-lost friends.

Sue O'Donnell

Memory Study II

Identify a specific event that happened at least a decade ago and included four other people from your past who you can still contact. Ask them to write down their memory of that specific event in as much detail as possible. Do not discuss or share your memories of the event with each other. Ask them to seal their memory in an envelope and mail it to you. Do not open the envelopes. Schedule a time when all four of you can be together, virtually or face to face. Then open and read aloud the four memories.

Sue O'Donnell
Memory Study III

Search for an address book from your past. Select five people that you have lost touch with. Find them and reconnect.

Claire B. Marcus
rePLACEments

rePLACEments: Restoring presence for the lost and displaced mentioned in the Domesday Book.

Assemble the names of all those dispossessed by the Norman Conquest, as recorded in the Domesday Book. Create a papercutting for each as a frame for light projected onto a particular abandoned landscape. Repeat every October 14th, the anniversary of the Battle of Hastings. Create pochoir prints from the cuttings, with the positive forms assembled into a book, then file the papercuttings within for future projections.

Cathryn Miller/Byopia Press

The Barbie Pictorial History of Western Art

At first glance, a perfectly average picture book of Western Art beginning with the Venus of Willendorf. At second glance, it is obvious that every female figure is based on a Barbie Doll.

Vera Benschop
Interference

This book is for film photographers who scan and dust their own images. Shoot a 35mm roll of 24–36 images (depending on how long you want the book to be) of whatever you choose. Develop the film and scan it — but don't dust it off as you scan. Edit images as usual including spot-dusting in photoshop. Sequence images. Go back to photoshop and remove the base layer, leaving only the areas that were retouched for dust (or any other reason). Print that.

Merridawn Duckler

Big Book of Nothing

Obtain large wood boards. Can be old doors. Modify them so they are the height and width of your body. Tear paper sheets. Lay down on one. Have someone you love, but do not altogether trust, roughly trace the outlines of your body, similar to an exercise once a staple of kindergarten crafts. Roll this tightly. With the following collaborators make more rolls, varying your position as needed.

someone you love who is indifferent
someone who loves you but is uneasy
someone with whom your love is reciprocal
someone with whom your love is problematic
someone who loves you disrespectfully
someone who is inconstant in their love
someone who is unconditional in their love
someone who only desires you physically
someone who is detached from your love
someone who represents your ideal of love
someone who is disdainful of all love
someone who loves you without effort
someone who destroys your love
someone who loves you as long as the body lasts

Roll tightly and use them in a piano hinge binding, with the boards holding "life-size" sheets of blank paper. Stand the book upright. Insert yourself into the book. Nothing is in the book.

Levi Sherman

Extended Family

Create an album of family photos that includes every family that has lived in your house. Request photos from former inhabitants and their descendants, then share the final book with them.

Imagination

Gwendolyn Paradice and Kyle Paradice

This is Not a Fairytale

This is Not a Fairytale invites readers to consider how the fantastical worlds of fairytales may be undermined by the standard printing of the books in which they appear. In an interconnected tale that spans six main characters over thousands of years, this novella-as-envisioned is a printer's nightmare (or dream).

The body of the protagonist is tattooed to resemble the map of the fairytale land she occupies. As she moves, the space her body mirrors moves as well. An arm up over her head: the musician's district in the capitol is transported to the mountains. One foot laying atop another: farms are drowned by the sudden appearance of a lake. Without consistency, entire cities and countries face ruin.

Pages are not turned; they are unfolded. As the reader progresses through the story, the "book" becomes the protagonist's skin-map. One large map becomes dozens of smaller maps. One "book" becomes a body, ever shifting. "Pages" of the text may be folded back in the way they originally appeared, or readers might choose to change the literal shape of the narrative and protagonist's body by experimenting with how, and when, text and image appear.

Narges Porsandekhial
Nothing and Everything

You enter an empty room. There's a 5 × 3.5 in. book and a pencil on the floor. The book has a red velvet cover but no title. The first page asks if you are willing to participate. If you continue, each page is filled with random words, tightly clustered on the paper in a surprisingly small font. On each page, in the middle of the pile, lies a different word. The last page of the book reveals this, and asks you to find those words. When you do, the book asks you to write a sentence, or even a short story using those words. You can write on the blank pages at the end of the book. You'll see different stories there, from different people, different minds, different conflicts and problems. It's your choice to participate, to be the author.

Amanda D'Amico
The Future of the Past

A timeline-inspired, landscape-oriented book that tracks the development of space travel and exploration in real life as compared to the timeline of progress in various science fiction films and television.

The original Lost in Space television series began with the United States sending the first family into space to live and to begin colonizing other planets. It was the year 1997.

The exploration of the universe in the Star Trek franchise relies on "warp drive" technology that allows ships to travel faster than light speed. Look forward to that innovation in 2063.

Battlestar Galactica has all happened before, and it will happen again in an endless loop of civilizations, born and destroyed. So what part of the loop are we in? How soon will our machines become sentient? One hundred years from now? Tomorrow? We may never know.

The book will be black with day-glo ink and can only be viewed in a basement with a few beanbags and a black light.

Sumru Tekin

A Manual for Collecting in Three Chapters (as told to Ü) Or Impossible Directions/Unnatural Disasters*

* five piles of text on a flat surface — single sheet of glass resting on five piles — you take turns to read aloud

I — The Arabian Nights, Mr. Mahdi, Borges, and me

uncompleted thought · single post-it note · Tolstoy translator's preface · alternate context she said

II — You walk into a bar. Bartender asks what'll it be? You say surprise me. Bartender does.

notes on · here there is an arrow pointing · notes on paper napkin · it is not called Turkish coffee in Armenian households · note to self

II — Girl walks into a bar Bartender asks what will it be Girl says nothing

circle drawn around these six words · you could even start here · things we have done things we haven't done things to do a to do list my grocery list don't forget the coffee · repeating a word until it loses its original meaning and is released to become something else

III — English is my second language

something appropriated taken from someone else ·
poem unknown

Epilogue: Bartender asks what'll it be? Surprised, we find ourselves thinking the same thing.

Translated from the Turkish by N. Aksakal

Peter and Donna Thomas

Ignited

This book is a series of photographs of a book being burned. The final product is the match box containing the ashes of the book.

Esther K Smith & Susan Happersett
Random Color Generated Instant Book

Supplies:

paper twice as long as wide

scissors

pencil

color mediums: red, yellow, blue,
white, medium gray, black

pair of dice

Fold an Instant Book:

fold paper in half lengthwise

open and fold in half crosswise

bring open end up to fold

turn over and bring other open end up to fold forming a W

from the peak to the valley of the W, cut a slit on
the crease from the original lengthwise fold

grasp each side of slit

turn hands and push together

finagle into a book

Open book to show grid

Throw dice — Combine the two colors in any way you like. You could mix them or paint/draw a design using your two colors — or do both.

Note — it is possible to get the same color twice on a page.

Dice numbers = these colors

1 Red

2 Yellow

3 Blue

4 White

5 Grey

6 Black

Fill each square of the grid
with indicated colors

When dry, repeat process on other side

When dry, fold back into instant book

Turn the pages

Marianne Dages

Dreamt I was reading The Book of Tides.

Dreamt I was reading *The Book of Tides.*

The pages were violet, white, and gray.

Onion skin.

The fore-edge of the book descended diagonally.

Like a pyramid's wall.

Nathanael Kooperkamp

Future Memory Photo Album

I want a book that is filled with the memories of my grandchildren. This book will contain their first times hosting Christmas, their happiness, their sorrow. Instead of grandchildren looking at photo albums of their grandparents, I would like the reverse to be possible. I would like a window into the lives I have touched but will never witness. I want their forgotten memories, their important moments. This feeling of nostalgia for something I have not experienced is something I want to put on my shelf. To stumble upon a pile of negatives that were never printed just to know that the moment in time was fixed. I do not have children yet, but this book would assure me that they have a future.

Safwat Saleem

The Self-Help Library

A book consisting of a collection of oddly specific and entirely imaginary self-help books that I wish had existed to guide me through parts of my life. Each page would be a photograph of a different book from the collection.

Esar Aadil

Dances of Great Contemplation

Make a book reminiscent of a glossy coffee table photobook of floral arrangements, with a cover that suggests as much. The reader will experience surprise as they flip through the book to find, on each page, no florals but exclusively photos of the movements involved in amateur floral arrangement. Include a variety of peoples' stance, balance, reach and stillness while they select flowers at a stand, shop, or even in the wild. The images will create the necessary context needed to colour the imaginative bouquet revealed to the reader by the reader.

Sydney Anne Smith

make a book like a dog

every good book is a dog. every book with teeth and tail wagging. make a book like a dog. the ones that gnash at your arms and stick their noses into crotches and lick at your toes. a lovely biting breathing thing. take a dog but don't shrink it down. it is only proper to use the full animal. or maybe you let it gestate into a bigger dog with fangs where the fur used to be, which can be the proper way but not always. take a book and tug at the edges until it takes to standing. pull at the paws until they extend into properly pointed talons. do not harness it or leash it or collar it if this can be avoided. do not give it a name tag either. do not let it sleep at the foot of your bed or eat any scraps from the table. now it is more coyote than dog and it shrieks and yowls like a frightened child. it can bite off your finger like a baby carrot, just like that, but it won't. it just howls until you draw nearer. the book, like the dog, is a bard, and you are its pupil in howling. face against fur, that is the right way to listen. cut your leg at the knee and let it gnaw at the bones. a dog like this will only take what it's given.

John Clark

Nothing Will Ever Suffice (unsatisfactory working title for this realisation only)

This book, without title, has been in the offing for as long as I have been writing, so a little over 30 years.

Whenever I see, read, or imagine a great book title, I often think that nothing more is needed. The title says it all. Nothing disappoints more than a poor book under a great title. From such high anticipation comes such a mighty fall. Why did the author not stop at the title? Leave the rest to the reader's imagination.

In its earliest incarnation, this idea for a book involved thinking up and noting down all manner of natty titles, neat names, the great and good in the imaginary mindscape of book titles. As my list grew long enough to make a small book, one question saw the project falter and eventually grind to a halt. What do you call a book of great titles? Surely a book that is nothing more than a list of imaginary book titles necessitates the greatest title of all.

And this conundrum remains to this day. In the absence of the greatest title of all, this book of great titles remains unrealised, a homage to all those great titles that have never come to pass, never come into being, remain pending at the title stage: unrealised potential in an unrealised project.

Connor Frew
Rat King

An anthology of short obituaries, killing the worst of the world in fiction — detailing their miseries, failings, violences, and deaths — featuring such luminaries as Elon Musk, Erik Prince, Warren Buffet, Henry Kissinger, et al. This dirge — not for its subjects but their victims — becomes so swollen and sharp that the rat king is assured of their own pitiful, spitting death. The book is added to, through public inquiry, programming, and public submission, until a communist revolution is crystallized through the process of elimination.

E.L. Gamble

Genocide Incorporated

One Universe. One Purpose. One People.

An alien corporation offers humanity's leaders the technology to fix Earth's problems in exchange for the marginalized portion of the population.

Genocide Incorporated is the journal of one of the exchanged humans, now employed by the alien corporation. Written in the margins of the official employee handbook, the story follows the character's emotional descent as they rise to become Executive Officer over Earth.

Shannon Davis
Wish You Were Here

Imagine a book of just the backs of postcards. As the viewer, you have no visual reference, only the written salutation, location, and your own imagination. The most banal of images, the cliché and expected, those that sacrifice depth of thought for the quickness of connection, are absent. Instead, these markings are the hieroglyphics to engagement, where the reader's mind can make connection. The written clues transport you into a moment the writer wishes you could be a part of. You both envision something different but together it becomes something new, something shifting, possibly lenticular — the image, a conceptual postcard that might compel you to say, "Wish you were here."

Carley Gomez

Operation Bird Book

Buy a notebook. Glue bird seed onto every page, so it can't be removed. Put on a Trump mask and take the book outside. Open it to the first page and set it on your doorstep. Make sure the crows see what you've done. At the end of the day, take the book back inside. No birds will have been able to eat the seeds. Repeat this ritual daily. Take the book on vacation and repeat the activity wherever you go.

Repeat this until you run out of pages and the crows have learned your "face." Read a different book while you wait for the crows to take action.

Andrew David King
Dickinson's Watch

An editioned artist's book of sequential poems produced in one of two variations. First variation: The sequence is entered into an algorithm which slightly rearranges the order of some of the poems' lines — though not the order of the poems — for each book, leaving no two books in the edition alike. The original is then destroyed. Second variation: Several versions of each poem in the sequence exist, all of which are entered into an algorithm that produces a unique sequence and combination of the poems for each book, leaving no two books in the edition alike. The original is then destroyed.

Kyle Adam Kalev Peets

A List of Things You Could Be Doing Right Now Instead of Reading This Book

Talk to a kid
Walk through a forest
Sort your elastic bands
Cook food
Close your eyes
Steal something
Describe the sky to a tree
Listen to see if the tree understands
Listen more
See how long you can walk with your eyes closed
See how long you can drive with your eyes closed
Go grocery shopping
Pressure-wash your shed
Grip a lantern
Face what you fear most
Listen to the trees again
Play a game that makes you run after someone
Call mom
Find your favorite shape
Organize the extra napkins you save from takeout

Wait for a really windy day and go out when it's windiest
and open your body so the wind goes right through you

Alyssa Laurel Ringler
Wall Street

When I started documenting Wall Street in 2009, 3% of Fortune 500 CEOs were women. The needle hasn't exactly shot forward. After 13 years, the number hovers between 6–8%, and only 6 are women of color.

In *Wall Street*, every photo I've taken on the floor of the NYSE is reenacted by an all-women cast. Colorful, glossy, full spreads of women Designated Market Makers, women traders, women shouting, women running, women running an IPO price discovery, women bankers hovering, women security, women press photographers photographing women CEOs, women on the Bell Podium with one token male assistant amongst C-Level women colleagues, women giving toasts in the Board Room, women signing the Distinguished Guests Book, women looking distressed, stressed, or angry, women staring off into space, women throwing trash on the Trading Floor after they've eaten their lunch, standing, in heels. I want to be surrounded by hundreds of sweaty women shouting and then cheering at the open of the biggest IPO in NYSE history. I want to see every moment I've captured represented only by women and I want every little girl to see this book, at home on a coffee table.

AB Gorham

UFO Song

Of UFOs but not extraterrestrials. The book's covers bulge toward the head with the shape of a UFO hovering, cast in resin and covered in bookcloth that has been letterpress printed from sky blue to desert floor brown and orange. There is a slit in the cloth exposing iridescent foil, illuminating the spacecraft. The reader/viewer is enchanted by this. There are no revelations as the first spread yawns open, only mystery as text shifts in scale from 42-line Gothic wood type letters to digital all-caps DIN typeface, creating strange object-combinations that float above the horizon in the reader/viewer's brain. The stiffness of the drumleaf spreads, in combination with the propped covers, leads the reader/viewer to engage both hands when handling this book. Each spread contains a vaguely-familiar visual mystery, letterpress printed in colors from saturated reds and golds to transparent violets. The text in the book, densely poetic and fragmented, follows a throughline of voice that flexes into Transcriptionist, Jokester, Witness. There is sidewalk cheese, lenticular clouds, and a landscape of crumbs. There is reassurance that what the reader/viewer sees is in fact real. The book ends with a silver landing.

Afterword

India Johnson

Afterword

Guide to Mail Standards of the United States Postal Service Domestic Mail Manual (DMM) Section 170

This guide definitively answers the question "What is a book?" We aim to end debate, once and for all, about the nature of the book, by referring all book inquiries to Section 170 of the Domestic Mail Manual: Media Mail and Library Mail.

For the convenience of the general public, as well as specialists — such as artists and writers — who work in book form, we include summaries of the most relevant subsections of section 170 below.

Last updated: 20 March 2020

Section	Summary	Prompt
1.0–1.1	Prices and Fees for Books: Media Mail prices and Library Mail prices are charged per pound or fraction thereof; any fraction of a pound is considered a whole pound.	If a book does not weigh 1 pound, it still costs 1 pound. To take full advantage of the minimum postage price per book, increase the weight of an existing book until it weighs 1 pound. Photograph the 1-pound book-object.
1.2	According to Notice 123—Price List, at minimum, a book may cost $2.67. At maximum, a book may cost $39.87.	Re-price an extant book by weight, rounded to the nearest pound. Offer it for sale to the public.
1.3.1-1.3.3	Instructions to determine single-piece weight in a mailing of identical-weight pieces.	Randomly sample 10 pieces [pieces of books or pieces of texts]. Weigh all the pieces and divide by the number of pieces. Round the average weight to two decimal places. Identify an item which approximates the average weight per piece. Affix the correct postage for the weight increment to the item, and mail the item. The mailed item is a book.

Section	Summary	Prompt
2.0	General Content Standards for Books: only mailable matter not entered as Periodicals meets standards of section 170.2.	Periodicals are not books. If a book you have made exhibits intention to serialize, attempt to authorize your book as a Periodical, using section 207.5.0, Applying for Periodicals Authorization. If you are unsure whether your book qualifies as a Periodical, write a definition of 'Periodical' using DMM Section 207.6.0, Periodical Qualification Categories. Note that this Guide does not cover Section 207.6.0.
3.0–3.1	Content Standards for Books: 3.1.a. books must consist of at least eight pages. The pages must be printed. Only reading matter is allowed on the pages. Comic books do not meet these standards.	Make a book of eight pages. The pages must be able to be read. The pages should include incidental blank spaces for notations.
	3.1.b. 16-mm or narrower width films are Books. So are catalogs of such films.	Make a book which catalogs a film. Note that this guide does not define 'film.' The catalog must include 24 pages (at least 22 of which are printed).
	3.1.c. Printed music, in bound or sheet form, is a Book.	If you have never made a book of printed music, do so now.

Section	Summary	Prompt
	3.1.d. Printed objective test materials used to test ability, aptitude, achievement, interests, or other mental and personal qualities are Books.	Compose a quiz. The quiz should be as objective as possible. Mail the quiz to ten people. Alternatively, mail the quiz to ten books. With or without answers, the quiz qualifies as a book. Collect and exhibit the responses you receive. (To calculate the price per piece of the mailing, consult subsections 1.1.1–1.1.3).
	3.1.e. Sound recordings are classified as Books.	Record a book breathing.
	3.1.f. Playscripts and manuscripts for books, periodicals, and music are Books.	Rewrite an extant text as a play. Play script with the text. Re-make a printed book as a manuscript. Re-make any book as music. Play the music to a book.

Section	Summary	Prompt
	3.1.g. Printed educational references charts are Books.	Make a chart. The chart is a book. Although according to 3.1.a, books must be eight pages, the chart must be a single sheet. The information may be printed on one or both sides, and it must be conveyed primarily by graphs, diagrams, tables, or other nonnarrative matter. A reference chart is normally, but not necessarily, devoted to one subject. Examples of charts which qualify as books include maps, tables of equations, tables of noun declensions or verb conjugations, periodic tables of the elements, and botanical or zoological tables.
3.2	Enclosures in Books	Enclose a book. Photograph the book in its enclosure, or outside of its enclosure. Is the book enclosed temporarily or for life? When is a book dead? Remember to feed the book regularly.

Section	Summary	Prompt
	3.2.a. Either one envelope or one addressed postcard may be bound into the pages of a book.	Make a book with one addressed postcard. The reader should want to return it to you. Bind one envelope into the pages of an extant book. Will you seal the envelope? Make a book using only one envelope. (If you use more than one envelope, your book does not qualify as a book. You will not be able to mail it as such, and must resort to delivery by hand. If you do not ship, what is the cost of handling?)

Section	Summary	Prompt
	3.2.b. One order form may be bound into the pages of a book.	Make an order form for an object or noun, concrete or abstract. To generate a book, order the form to noun. Is a form a book? Is the book a form? For three weeks, record all your form sightings in a notebook. After this inventory of forms, write an order form for form, allowing readers to order the particular forms they would like to read. Be sure to include a price with each form and to love the reader. What is a book? Forms to order. If also serving as an envelope or postcard, the form may be in addition to the envelope or card permitted by 3.2.a. Finally, make a book in postcard form.
	3.2.c. Announcements of books may appear as book pages. These announcements must be incidental and exclusively devoted to books. Up to three such announcements are permitted per book.	Write announcements for three hypothetical books. Announcements must fully describe the conditions and methods of each book, and contain ordering instructions. What happens when the reader orders? What happens when the reader is a menu item?

Section	Summary	Prompt
4.1	Sender and Recipient Qualifications	Survey your friends, acquaintances, and enemies about their reading habits (social media is an excellent methodology for reaching all three groups). Identify one person who does not read. Mail them a book. Make three lists of books: one for friends, one for enemies, and one for ghosts.
4.2	Content Standards for Mailing Between Entities: The items described in this section may be mailed at the Library Mail price when sent between: (1) schools, colleges, universities, public libraries, museums, and herbariums and nonprofit religious, educational, scientific, philanthropic, agricultural, labor, veterans, and fraternal organizations or associations or (2) any such institution and a publisher.	Pose as a school of, college of, university of, or as a museum of. Pose as a public library. You are full of books. Pose as an herbarium. You are full of plants. You are a nonprofit religious, educational, scientific, philanthropic, or agricultural organization. You are a labor organization. On behalf of this organization, author a book. Send it to a publisher. Plants are books.
4.3	Museum materials, specimens, collections, scientific or mathematical kits, instruments, or other devices are books.	Mail one such book. If it breaks in the post, see subsection 1.1.1–1.1.3. (summary) to calculate the average price per piece.

Section	Summary	Prompt
4.4	Enclosures in Books and Sound Recordings	Enclose something in sound. Where is the book? The book is enclosed. Close the book.
	4.4.c. Books and sound recordings mailed at the Library Mail price may contain announcements on title labels, protective sleeves, on the carton or wrapper, or on loose enclosures.	Make a book that is a series of labels. Protect the book.
5.0	Basic Eligibility Standards for Books	Make three books: a basic book, a standard book, and an eligible book. Date the eligible book.
5.1	The USPS does not guarantee the delivery of books within a specified time.	Make a book that will no longer exist when it arrives. Make a book that will not exist. Make a book that is not guaranteed within a specified time. Make a book that is guaranteed to be specific. Make a system for guaranteeing reading.
5.2	Mailings of books must bear a delivery address and the sender's return address.	Mail a book to a non-address. When the book is returned to sender, photograph the book. Affix fresh postage. Remail the book. Gradually you will become the book's sole reader. However, you must never read its texts.

Section	Summary	Prompt
5.3–5.4	Inspection of contents: The mailing of books at Media Mail or Library Mail prices constitutes consent by the mailer to postal inspection of the contents.	Make a book which is able to consent to an inspection of its contents. Make a book whose contents are able to consent to inspection. Make a book which is unable to consent to an inspection of its contents. Make an inspection procedure for books, regardless of their consent. Make a trial procedure for those who violate a book's consent.
5.5	All books mailed must bear an Intelligent Mail package barcode.	Switch the barcodes of two library books. Why these two books? Switch the barcodes of every book in a library.
6.0	Enclosures and Attachments	Attach something to a book. Photograph the book and its attachment. The attachment should not interfere with postal processing. Mail the attachment, but not the book.

Section	Summary	Prompt
6.1	An invoice may be placed inside a book, or attached to the outside of the piece if it relates solely to the matter with which it is mailed.	Before reading a book, invoice the book. On your invoice, include the name and address of the author and the reader, and the estimated quantity of the articles enclosed in the book or text, with descriptions of each (including the price, tax, style, stock number, size and quality, and nature of defects). Place the invoice in an envelope marked "Invoice Enclosed" and attach it to the outside of the book. After reading, pay the invoice.
6.2	Incidental Enclosures in Books	Make sure every book you mail includes a bill for its publication, or a statement of account for past publications, enclosed in the book. You are accountable for all your past publications. The reader is accountable for the bill.
6.3	Loose Enclosures: Any printed matter may be included loose with any qualifying mailed book.	Make a book with an equal amount of bound and loose matter. Unbind a book. Reorder the book. Rebind the book. Do not follow best book conservation practices.

Section	Summary	Prompt
6.4	Written Additions: Markings that have the character of personal correspondences require additional postage, beyond book prices. The following exceptions apply: 6.4.a. "From," "To," and directions for handling 6.4.b. Marks, numbers, names, or letters describing the contents 6.4.c. Words or phrases such as "do not open" and "happy birthday, mother" 6.4.d. Instructions and directions for the use of the book mailed 6.4.e. A manuscript dedication or inscription 6.4.f. Marks to call attention to words or passages in the text 6.4.g. Corrections of typographical errors in printed matter 6.4.h. Manuscripts accompanying proofs including corrections of errors, changes in the text, insertions, or new text, marginal instructions to the printer, and corrective rewrites of parts 6.4.i. Hand-stamped imprints	Wrap eight books. On the outside, leave written instructions. The books should still be mailable as books. After addressing the books, mail them.

Section	Summary	Prompt
7.0-7.1	Basic Weight Standards: There is no minimum weight for books. A single book can weigh no more than 70 pounds.	Make a book that is as light as possible. You may start from scratch or with an extant book. If working from an extant book, you must preserve all its information. Make a book that weighs 70 pounds. Carry the book for as long as it takes to read.
7.2	Price Eligibility Standards: A presorted book mailing must contain at a minimum, 300 pieces.	To make a single book eligible for mass mailing, you must separate it into 300 pieces. The pieces may be as small as a character, or as large as a word. Spaces between words do not count. This is for the same reason that a book is not more than its specific weight.
7.3	Prices to mail books are based on the weight of the piece without regard to zone.	Weigh several books and write reviews of them based on their weight and volume. The reviews should disregard zone, text, paratexts, signs, images, tables, diagrams, charts, and numbering systems. The reviews should disregard the author. They should disregard the reader, who has never loved you.
7.3.1	Flats	Flatten a book: make the entire book visible on a single plane.

Section	Summary	Prompt
7.3.2	Parcels	Parcel a book: mail the appropriate parts of a book to the appropriate people. Mail the appropriate parts of people to the appropriate books.
7.3.2.a-7.3.2.d	Non-machinable Parcels	Sort a series of books by hand. What is the difference between a stack and a pile? What is the difference between a pile and a list? What is the difference between a list and a book?

If you have doubts about whether a book you have made is eligible for Media and Library Mail prices, please send your inquiry to India Johnson, care of Partial Press. In order for your inquiry to be considered, use form A (Book Doubt Form).

If you wish to document the outcome of any of the above prompts, use form B (Book? Form).

If you wish to contest any of the above guidelines for book eligibility, please contact the United States Postal Service with your inquiry.

If you wish to create a similar Guide to the requirements for mailing books outside of the United States, please inform the head postmaster, India Johnson.

Form A: Book Doubt Form

Choose one:

I, _______________ (you), am

[ ] reader of books

( ) the reader

( ) a Writer

[ ] Of poetic texts

[ ] Of fictional texts

[ ] Of poetic books

[ ] Of fictional books

[ ] writer, other: __________________

[ ] an Editor of texts

[ ] a Maker of books

[ ] a Publisher of books

[ ] a Collector of books

[ ] a Cataloger of books

( ) a book

( ) a b c d e f g h i j k l m n o p q r s t u v w x y z

[ ] a ________________

harbor doubts as to whether my book, ____ (insert book), qualifies as a book for postal purposes, as outlined by Guide to the Mail Standards of the United States Postal Service Domestic Mail Manual (DMM) Section 170 ________________ (insert subsection).

(Articulate your book doubts in the box below:)
Book
Doubt
box

- -

For postmaster use only:
[ ] This is a book
[ ] This is a Book
[ ] This is not a book
[ ] This is a text
[ ] This is not a text, but this is a book
[ ] This is a book, conditional upon: _______________

Contributors

Aadil, Esar 148
Alsop, Maureen 95
Benschop, Vera 71, 130
Bruex, Ellen 99
Byopia Press. See Miller, Cathryn
Carcia, Karen 98
carter, derrais 34
Cearley, S 55
Clark, John 150
Croxson, Marcel 45
Dages, Marianne 145
D'Amico, Amanda 139
Davis, Shannon 153
Dreamer, Nada 47
Drysdale, Bea 112
Duckler, Merridawn 131
Elliott, Reba 64
Ernst, K.S. 76
Falcone, Karin 110
Feist, Judith Caroline 108
Freid, Carol 35
Frew, Connor 41, 114, 115, 151
Gamble, E.L. 152
Gelman, Annelyse 48
Gialanella, John 106
Gomez, Carley 17, 154
Gorham, AB 158
Guidry, Abigail 97
Hampton, Michael 105
Hanson, Alex 49
Happersett, Susan 143
Harris, Susanna 69
Henry, Rick 51
HER(GEHOLT), VON WEIT 39
Irons, Bethanie 52
Johnson, Bethany 42
Johnson, India 161
Jones, Nathanael 44
Kassianidou, Marina 107
King, Andrew David 77, 79, 81, 116, 155
Kobelt, Catalina 50
Kohlmann, Lui 43
Kooperkamp, Nathanael 146
Kreiser, Constanze 53
Lee, Bobby 29

Leslie, Woody 74
Liu, Florence Lanxuan 80
Lyle, Kristen 104
Mairs, Will 65
Maker, Sarah 85
Maloney, Evan Patrick 73
Marcus, Claire B. 128
Marin, Meghan 113
Mati 40
M H 123
Miller, Cathryn 30, 46, 68, 129
Monica The Creative Beast 83
Nabarra, Amandine 101, 117
Neiva, Bruno 82
O'Donnell, Sue 125, 126, 127
Oeftering, Liz 78
Oliver, Lily 124
ossa 121
Paradice, Gwendolyn 137
Paradice, Kyle 137
Parr, Linda 119
Peets, Kyle Adam Kalev 156
Petrauskas, Katrina 57
Porsandekhial, Narges 88, 138
Powers-Torrey, Marnie 56, 86
Ramos, Eileen 66
Ribière, Mireille 118
Ringler, Alyssa Laurel 157
Robinson, Lisa Beth 89
Ruda, Lesley 90
Saleem, Safwat 147
Sherman, Gabriel 33, 58
Sherman, Levi 31, 32, 133
Smith, Esther K 143
Smith, Sydney Anne 149
Spencer, Kyla Anne 91
Spyker, James 37, 38, 72
Stablein, Marilyn 75
Tekin, Sumru 140
Thomas, Donna 142
Thomas, Peter 142
We Da Pepo 62
Whitehead, Morgan 122
Wylde, Nanette 92
Zlatar, Ally 102
Zorrilla, Karla 61

www.ingramcontent.com/pod-product-compliance
Lightning Source LLC
LaVergne TN
LVHW010700110826
845149LV00014B/3178

* 9 7 8 0 9 9 8 0 7 1 1 2 1 *